NINE DAYS IN SINGAPORE

A Family Affair
(With a Pitstop in Dubai)

NINE DAYS IN SINGAPORE

A Family Affair
(With a Pitstop in Dubai)

WARREN LANDRUM

Warland Books
Grand Prairie, Texas

NINE DAYS IN SINGAPORE
Published by:
Warland Books
2791 Explorador
Grand Prairie, TX 75054
Warrenglandrum@hotmail.com

Warren Landrum, Publisher / Editorial Director
Carol Landrum, Photo Editor
Yvonne Rose/Quality Press, Production Coordinator

ALL RIGHTS RESERVED No part of this book may be reproduced or transmitted in any form or by any means – electronic or mechanical, including photocopying, recording or by any information storage and retrieved system without written permission from the authors, except for the inclusion of brief quotations in a review.

Warland Books are available at special discounts for bulk purchases, sales promotions, fund raising or educational purposes.

© Copyright 2019 by Warren Landrum and Warland Books

Paperback ISBN #: 978-1-0878-0646-4
Ebook ISBN #: 978-1-7333195-1-5
Library of Congress Control Number: 2019911640

DEDICATION

This book is dedicated to all world-travelers, who seek to explore and understand other cultures in the spirit of establishing one true world-wide community of Peace.

ACKNOWLEDGEMENTS

I would like to thank my niece, Raech Gonzal, for all she did for us for this trip, which was pretty much everything. Raech extended the offer for my wife Carol and I to stay with her and her husband Bert and their 5-year old Yuan, in their condo in Northern Singapore, during our trip. This was most gracious and much appreciated.

Raech also planned and had laid out for us, day-by-day, all the activities and attractions that we would see and experience while in Singapore. Her planning ensured that we had a total immersion experience and were able to get a feel for Singapore and its many facets. This even included a recommendation for an overnight trip to an island in Indonesia.

PREFACE

Hello. Welcome to "Nine Days in Singapore: A Family Affair…" the 3rd book in my Travel series, following "Nine Days in Italy…" and "Nine Days in Paris…." I decided to write this book, because Singapore is not on the radar when people in the United States talk about must-see travel destinations, and it should be! Singapore is a very modern cosmopolitan city, with a Financial District rivaling Wall Street, and more importantly, it is a culturally diverse city where the influence of Malaysia, India, and China blends with the modern influences to create a City-State of unparalleled charms. Additionally, there is much to see and do in Singapore for a tourist, so I wholeheartedly recommend that you consider putting it on your list of future travel and vacation destinations. You will NOT be disappointed.

TABLE OF CONTENTS

Dedication i
Acknowledgements iii
Preface v
Table of Contents vii
I. Plan, Plan, Plan 1
II. August 3rd T-Minus 2 Months till Takeoff 3
III. September 5th T-Minus 30 Days till Arrival in Singapore 6
   In Singapore: 8
   In Malaysia: 9
IV. Pre-Dubai Planning 12
V. Let the Adventures Begin! 15
VI. Arrival in Dubai 17
VII. Dubai 19
   Burj Khalifa 19
   Burj Al Arab 25
   The Souks 30
VIII. Singapore… At Last! 32
IX. A Family Reunion 35
X. First Full Day 40
   The Merlion 41
   Gardens by The Bay 42
   The Flower Dome 43
   Cloud Forest 45

- Satay by the Bay 46
- Supertrees Grove 47

XI. Sunday is Funday! 51
- Orchard Road 51
- Changing of the Guard 53
- Spectra Light Show 57
- Marina Bay Sands Observation Deck 58

XII. Montigo Resort on Batam Island, Indonesia 61

XIII. Family Time with The Gonzals 68

XIV. Little India and the Mustafa Market 71
- Warren and Family Arrive 74

XV. October 11th My 64th Birthday 75
- Happy Birthday Serenade & Cake 75
- The Singapore Zoo 76
- Night Safari 79

XVI. Sentosa Island 81
- Sentosa Island 83

XVII. Our Last Full Day in Singapore 90
- S.E.A. Aquarium 91
- The Casino 95
- VivoCity Mall –Largest in Singapore 96
- Warren and Family Leave 97

XVIII. Sunday, October 14th The Journey is Over 98
- …But It's Not the End 101

Appendix A 103

Appendix B 104

Warren's Bio 105

1
PLAN, PLAN, PLAN

As those of you who have been along with me on the other books in the "Nine Days" series know, I really like to plan as much of the trip in advance as possible, in regard to itinerary and excursions or sight-seeing events. In Italy, we identified some of the "must-see" things like the Sistine Chapel and the Coliseum and Trevi Fountain in Rome and the statue of David in Florence, the Leaning Tower in Pisa, and the canals of Venice.

Then in Paris, through research, and from talking to friends before the trip, we found out about the Black Paris Walking Tours and the Monet Gardens and that purchasing a Paris Pass would be the best way for us to get around Paris via the Metro, bypassing the lines on some of the major attractions that we wanted to visit. We did extensive research before the trip to try and make sure that we maximized our time and saw everything that we really wanted to see once we got there.

Singapore will be different. There are no well-known worldwide attractions that come to mind when one thinks of Singapore. My pre-trip research thus far has found nothing that really jumps out at me as a "must-see" attraction. So, I basically put putting the itinerary together into the hands of my niece Raech, who we will be staying with. As I mentioned earlier, Raech is a fun-loving person and good at this type of thing, so I know we will be in good hands.

One of the first things she suggested was that we spend at least a day or two at one of the resorts on the beach in either Malaysia or Indonesia. She said that these were all within a 45-minute ferry ride, and since coming over to this part of the world from the United States was not cheap, we probably want to do, see, and experience as much as we can. So, she sent me information on a couple of the resorts that she and Bert had personally stayed in and recommend in those two countries, and after checking them out on the websites and reading various reviews from other folks, I reserved a night at Montigo Resort Nongsa, on Batam Island, Indonesia. We will actually be staying in a one-bedroom Villa on the beach, with our own private infinity pool as well. Sounds like fun!

II
AUGUST 3ʳᴰ
T-MINUS 2 MONTHS TILL TAKEOFF

Passports verified. Check!! Airline Reservations still good? Check!! Alrighty then...

Each vacation and each Travel Journey is uniquely different and takes on a life of its own. As we have done in our last two Travel books, "Nine Days in Italy: The Highs and Lows of Driving Through Italia" and "Nine Days in Paris: The Journey Continues," we will try to give you our insights into what some of the Dos and Don'ts and "Gotchas" for visiting Singapore may be, in addition to just allowing you to be the proverbial "fly on the wall" to tag along with us as we experience some of the adventures and locales and events that await us.

This trip will have more of a Family Spin on it, I am sure. We will be staying with my niece Raech Gonzal and her husband Bert, and their 5-year old son Yuan, in their condo in Singapore, so that will be our base for our adventures. Raech is one of two Filipino Nieces and two Nephews that I have, as a result of my Dad's romantic encounter during World War II with a young Filipina he encountered while stationed over in the Philippines. That union produced one son, Rodolfo "Warren" Fernandez, my late big Half-Brother.

I got to meet my brother around 20 years ago, when I used to travel back and forth to Bangkok on job assignments for the semi-conductor company that I worked for at the time. I later met Raech, as she traveled from Manila, to spend some time over in Bangkok with my wife Carol and me. Raech and Bert later came out to visit us in Phoenix and we took them up to the Grand Canyon.

But the occasion on which I met my Brother was very joyful and emotional. I remember when I was a little kid, he had sent letters to my parents, asking, I guess, if there was any way he could join us in the States. I remember my mother showing me some of those letters, including some with pictures of him in his police uniform. But obviously, he never joined us in the States, and he wound up getting married in the Philippines and starting a family of his own, which eventually came to consist of four children – my only nieces and nephews.

So, when I arrived at Manila airport and saw him coming toward me in his uniform, there was no doubt! He looked JUST LIKE My Dad, big Landrum nose and all! He wrapped a Big, tearful Bear-Hug around me, and just started saying, "Brother, My Brother," over and over. After we finished our embrace, all the kids ran up to hug me as well. Again, it was quite an emotional scene right there at the airport.

When they got me to their home, there was a big banner, made out of Computer Printer Paper, attached to the wall. It said, "Welcome Uncle Warren." It was so moving, and I swelled up knowing that I now had more family I could call my own.

I spent about three or four days with the Family in the Pasig City part of the Manila Metroplex, and they took me around the country showing me various things of interest. Some of the highlights included when we went on a drive into the country and visited a village where they had replicas of some of the various different types of buildings and things that showcased the culture, history, and traditions of the people. My brother also called one of his friends over, and we had a session of drinking Filipino Whiskey and eating 1000-year-old eggs (well, they ate, I watched, and tried not to throw up!)

So, by the time we got done with all this familial bonding, I really felt great. I also knew that my little niece Raech is a great tour guide. Raech and Bert have a 5-year old now, and my nephew, Warren, will be coming over to join us from the Philippines, with his wife and 3-year old son, as will my other nephew, Miko. Can't wait to see The Fam again!

III
SEPTEMBER 5TH
T-MINUS 30 DAYS TILL ARRIVAL IN SINGAPORE

Well, this was a good day for the Planning aspect of the trip. Last week, at work, we received an e-mail announcement that a new Director had been hired in our IT Department, the department in which I work. I started reading through his Bio, and the following words jumped out at me – "Prior to making Dallas his home, Subbu lived in India, Singapore, and Malaysia." Whoa! Another resource for Singapore information. I jumped all over it!

I sent Subbarao Saladi - "Subbu," his abbreviated name- an e-mail immediately, welcoming him to the company, introducing myself, and telling him that I would be going over to Singapore on vacation for about nine or ten days in October, and I asked him if I could drop by to get some insight as to what to check out over there. He IMMEDIATELY replied to my e-mail, and told me, 'Sure' – to drop on by whenever I got a chance, and he'd be glad to share with me. I thanked him and told him that I worked from home the remainder of the week, but I would check him out when I got back in the office after Labor Day.

We were both on the same floor at work (the 24th floor of a 31-floor office building in downtown Dallas) so I cruised by his office when I got settled in on Tuesday. He was not there the first few times I walked by, and the next couple of times, he had someone in the office. So, I decided to just give him another shot the next day – today.

I finally found him in his office after lunch and peeked in and introduced myself – telling him I was the guy who was going to Singapore next month. His face immediately softened, and he welcomed me in. He checked his calendar, because he said he wanted to make sure that he did not have any meetings coming up that would have to cut our chat short. He didn't and so he offered me a seat and I settled in. He had an easy smile and manner about him, and I felt right at home at once!

Subbu was actually more, or at least equally, excited about my upcoming trip, as I was. He said that when I sent him the e-mail, it gave him the opportunity to reflect on some of the good memories and experiences that he had when he lived over in Singapore and Malaysia. We chatted for almost an hour and he gave me a whole list of things that I might want to check out, pulling them up on the Internet on his desktop as we went along.

For the sake of giving you a concise reference location in case you ever have the opportunity to visit Singapore, I am going to list some of the spots and activities he mentioned. I will list the ones in Singapore first, and then the ones in Malaysia.

In Singapore:

1) *Sentosa Island* – Underwater World and *Sea Aquarium*
2) Jurong Bird Park
3) *Orchard Road* – 2.2km strip of shops and restaurants
4) City Center
   a) *Marina Bay Sands Light Show* – 8pm
   b) Singapore Flyer Ferris Wheel – kind of like the Eye in London, only 30 meters taller
   c) *Gardens by the Bay*
   d) *Casino*
   e) Art-Science Museum
   f) Marina Bay Esplanade aka 'The Durian"
   g) Asian Civilization Museum

Note: The items above that are italicized are the ones from this list that we actually made it to during our trip...

In Malaysia:

1) Genting Highlands – Pahang, Malaysia
   (6.5hrs by bus, 75 minutes by air)
   a) Cable Car Ride
   b) Genting Theme Park
   c) Casino
2) Palace of the Golden Horses – in Kuala Lumpur
3) Batu Caves – Hindu Shrines and Temples in Kuala Lumpur
4) Petronas Towers – Kuala Lumpur: Tallest Twin Towers in the world – Tallest Building in the world from 1998-2004

These are some of the things and places that Subbu mentioned. You can Google any of these to get more info about them to see if they might fit into your plans.

One thing I found when I started Googling them, is that Kuala Lumpur is about an 8-hour drive from Singapore. You can also get there by train, which takes about 6.5 hours. There are three trains a day doing the Singapore-Kuala Lumpur route, including one night-train.

Malaysia Airlines can also get you from Singapore to Kuala Lumpur in about an hour.

As to the question of whether U.S. citizens need a Visa to get to Malaysia from Singapore, here is some info from the U.S. State Department's website:

To enter Malaysia:

- *Your passport must be valid for at least six months.*
- *You do not need a visa if you are coming for business or tourism for 90 days or less.*
- *Immigration officials will place an entry stamp, known as a social visit pass (visa), in your passport authorizing a stay of up to 90 days. Travelers may apply to the Immigration Department for extensions of up to two months*

So, the answer is, "No" you do not need a Visa or anything special to go to Malaysia from Singapore. But you definitely need to do some planning before heading up to Kuala Lumpur. It may even require an overnight stay in order to take your time and visit some of these attractions to get the full benefit of what makes each one an attraction.

Subbu also gave me a sense of how safe it is in Singapore. This is good to know for people like my wife, and for some of you, who may be a little leery when visiting foreign countries, or even different cities in the United States. He said it is totally safe, to the point where he had no qualms riding his bicycle to work at 2am in the morning! So, we can all rest easy on that point.

Subbu also told me about some of the "No-No's" that they take seriously and frown upon over there – things that can have serious penalties. You may have heard of some of these; things like No Spitting, No Chewing Gum, No Littering, and even No Smoking, unless it is Singapore-branded cigarettes. I know I have allergies here in the States that frequently cause me to expectorate, so I am definitely going to have to be aware of that and control that more once we get to Singapore!

IV
PRE-DUBAI PLANNING

I probably should have started this a little earlier, but after the initial online excursion that I just made, I believe we'll be alright.

Since we are going to have a 9-hour layover in Dubai, we obviously want to get out and explore the City and see as many of the "Must-See" sights as possible. The main ones on the list are Burj Khalifa, which is the world's tallest building currently, and Burj Al Arab, the famous 7-Star luxury hotel that sits on its own private man-made island.

A couple of the main items I needed to check in to were 1) what is the process for getting out of the airport and into the country and 2) What is the best way to get around to get from the airport into the city and to get around to the various sights we want to see.

Well, the answer to the first question involves Visa Status. Do we need to get a temporary Visa to be allowed to leave the airport and get into the city? I had not given this much thought and none of the folks that I had spoken to about our layover in Dubai said anything like "Make sure you get a Dubai Visa before you leave" or anything like that, so I had not checked on this. But I thought I'd better do so now, just to make sure. I was pleasantly surprised when I Googled "Layover in Dubai" and learned that if you were on one of the countries in a certain list, you did not need anything special to leave the airport and visit. All you needed to do was to go to the Immigration Desk and they would stamp your Passport giving you a Temporary Visa and it was Free! So that took care of THAT question!

As to how to physically get transportation from the airport and get into the city, there are several options that require a little more investigation. Let me go ahead and research those, and I'll be back with you in a few to delineate the options for you and tell you which ones I chose for us.

Okay, I'm back... After checking with a friend who had been to Dubai before, she suggested that, with the amount of time we had to spend there during our layover, that we should just book a tour. Oh, I hadn't thought of that. But how simple! I got online and Googled "Layover Tours in Dubai" and sure enough, I found one called "With Locals." I read the reviews in regard to this one particular tour guide who conducted these tours, and I have never seen such high marks and comments on any other review I have looked at before. Of the 169 Reviews, 166 were 5-Stars, two were 4-Stars, and one was 3-Stars. None were negative. So, I contacted the guide, Gomez, by WhatsApp to see if he was going to be available the day and time we were going to be in Dubai, and he was. So, I plopped down the

Credit Card payment, and just like that, the logistics of our Tour worries for Dubai was over. He would pick us up at the airport, show us around, and drop us back off at the airport. Now we were officially ready for our trip, as this was the last open item on my checklist!

V
LET THE ADVENTURES BEGIN!

We were just settling into our seats in Row 44 of our Emirates Airbus A300-600 (9 and 10-across seating in Economy Class), still parked at the gate, for our 14 hour and 45-minute flight from Dallas to Dubai, when the adventure started. We always know that there is going to be some unpredictable event or events that occur during the course of our vacations, but this one started a little early!

It started with a stewardess walking up and down the aisles asking if anyone had been given a laptop bag to carry on the plane with them. My first thoughts were BOMB, TERRORISTS! I then started thinking, "How can we get off this plane?" It's kind of crazy that that's where my mind went immediately, but when you think about the world we live in today, I guess it's not really so crazy after all. Carol and I sort of just looked at each other as she continued walking the aisles. After what seemed like an eternity, but was probably just a couple minutes, an Indian woman three rows in front of us, dressed in traditional Indian garb, said that she had carried on such a bag at someone's request. A couple more Airline Officials quickly approached her and asked her to leave the plane with them. At this point, she began freaking out and crying and such and would not leave, until after a bit of cajoling, the officials agreed to let what I'm guessing were her husband and son, accompany her off. They quickly exited the plane with her. Within minutes, other flight attendants came down the aisles, and for every piece of baggage in the overhead bins, they made sure there was an owner attached to it. Obviously they were checking to make sure that someone had not left an unescorted bag on the plane. This was scary stuff, straight out of a movie script.

Anyway, I guess each bag checked out with an owner, because we did not hear anything else and no further action was taken. And after about 15 or 20 minutes, the Indian woman and her family returned to their seats. I guess they had satisfied the authorities that they were not terrorists. Within a few more minutes, we were airborne, for our, thankfully, uneventful *(*3 Movies Watched = *Uncle Drew, Breaking In, and Iron Man 3*) almost 15-hour flight to Dubai. But what a start to our trip!

VI
ARRIVAL IN DUBAI

During the last two hours of the flight, they woke us up to serve us breakfast as part of the process of trying to get us acclimated to the time change. Dubai was 9 hours ahead of Dallas, so paired with the almost 15-hour flight, it was about 24 hours later when we landed in Dubai. We took off on Wednesday at around Noon and touched down around Noon on Thursday.

As soon as we were able to turn our cell phones back on, I turned mine on, and there was a WhatsApp message from our guide Gomez, along with a photo of him. He told us that he would meet us by a little coffee shop (their version of Starbucks) that we would pass as soon as we exited the Airport through the main exit.

We exited the plane and got to that area and he was not there. I pinged him with WhatsApp and he said he was caught in traffic, but sure enough, within about 10 more minutes, we saw his smiling face walking up to greet us. He escorted us back to the huge SUV (Carol could barely make the step to get inside) that was awaiting with the driver and away we went. Gomez was very engaging, and we instantly felt right at home and very comfortable with him. As the driver exited the airport, Gomez kind of laid out some of the things he had planned and then asked us if there was anything in particular that we wanted to see. But to be honest, he had pretty much covered all the things I had researched, so we just settled back into our seats and prepared for the sights and sounds of Dubai.

VII
DUBAI

Before I get going, let me tell you a little about Dubai logistically. Dubai is the capital city of the Emirate of Dubai, one of the seven emirates (emirates translates to "kingdoms") that make up the United Arab Emirates (UAE.) It is the largest city in the UAE and is located on the southeast coast of the Persian Gulf (currently referred to as the Arabian Gulf.)

Before talking about and showing you some of the many sights, some iconic, to see in Dubai, let me tell you a little bit about how I want to lay this section of the book out. Our guide, Gomez, was very helpful, and gave us a lot of little insights, background info, and cultural tidbits about some of the places we would be seeing and going to. So, where appropriate, I will present some of these to you. I just think it will make your trip a little more enjoyable, as you tag along with us. Sound Good? Cool!

Burj Khalifa

The first place that Gomez took us to was Burj Khalifa, by way of the Dubai Mall. Burj Khalifa is currently the tallest building in the world, but the Dubai Mall is no slouch as a place to visit either. It is the 2nd largest mall in the world, going by total land area, and it has over 1200 shops. In 2011, the Mall was the most visited building on the planet! It seems as though everything in Dubai is either the Biggest or the Tallest or the Best, or striving to be so!

We actually had to pass through the Mall to get to Burj Khalifa, so we got to see a little of it, and some of the attractions in it, one of which is the Dubai Aquarium and Underwater Zoo. The viewing panel which is one wall of the Aquarium is the World's Largest Acrylic Panel (surprise, surprise.)

Upon exiting the back end of the mall on the route to Burj Khalifa, the first thing you encounter upon stepping out into the hot, arid heat is The Dubai Fountain. It is (you guessed it) the World's Largest Choreographed Fountain System, with its dancing fountains and light show. It is in the middle of man-made Burj Khalifa Lake and it was designed by the same U.S. company that designed the fountains in front of the Bellagio Hotel in Vegas. We were fortunate enough to catch one of the afternoon performances of the fountain, and I'm sure the night-time shows must be pretty special, based on what we saw.

Before we get to Burj Khalifa itself, I have to tell you the story about how it got its name, as told to us by Gomez. The building was originally called Burj Dubai. Burj means

"Tower." After the financial crash of 2008, the Sheik and Ruler of Abu Dhabi and President of the United Arab Emirates – Khalifa bin Zayed Al Nahyan, donated $20 Billion US Dollars of his "pocket change" to allow Dubai to pay its debts. The building was then renamed Burj Khalifa in his honor when it was officially opened in 2010.

Quick Fact: 83% of Dubai's residents are foreigners.

Burj Khalifa
Tallest Building in the World!
2716.5 Feet, 163 Stories High

After seeing the Burj from the fountain area and watching the fountain show, we were anxious to get over to it, so that we could make our ascension to the Observation Deck. But we had to go around the corner and cross a small bridge to enter the mall at a different entry point to be able to get to the corridor that would lead us to the Tower.

Gomez parted ways from us in front of a candy store in the mall and told us he would be there when we returned, as he had purchased tickets for us to go to one of the Observation Decks. So, we bid him adieu, and got into the line that was formed past some stairs and onto a ramp that led up to the level where we would board the elevator. There was a tour group of about 20 or so folks in front of us who were getting a guided tour from their guide, and maybe about a couple dozen more people ahead of us.

Altogether, it took us about 20 or 30 minutes to get to the boarding point, which had some of those felt rope barriers, sort of like what they have in movie theaters in the States when you are waiting for the premier of a hot new movie. They were letting in about 20 or so folks at a time, as the elevator was a decent size. Once inside it, we were told that it would take us about 60 seconds to go the 124 floors to the Observation Deck that we would be disembarking at. That's pretty darn fast! The elevator started and the only way you could tell you were moving was by looking at the little square box that was keeping digital count and display the floors as we passed each one. It was quiet, smooth, and relatively dark, as there were no windows to the outside. At about floor number 40, my ears started popping like they do when you're ascending in an airplane, and before you knew it, we were there!

When we stepped off the elevator and onto the Observation Deck, the view was exhilarating! We looked out the windows and could see the full expanse of Dubai stretching out in front of us and way below us! The first thing I noticed was the symmetry and design of their main highway, which could be seen clearly from this 124th Floor view.

As we started making our way around the deck, it kind of reminded me of the view from up in the Eifel Tower in Paris, where you got a full panoramic view of the city as you walked the perimeter of the deck. Only this building is MUCH higher than the Eifel Tower! Burj Khalifa is about 163 stories, whereas the tip-top of the Eifel Tower is equivalent to about an 81-story building!

Cultural Lesson #1: If you see a couple Muslim men doing what looks like an act of Kissing in public, look closer. It is customary for Men to touch noses 3 times when greeting each other as a sign of respect!

After leaving Burj Khalifa, our next major destination was Burj Al Arab. But on the way there, we would encounter two more treasures of Dubai – The Frame, and the Ski Dubai SnowPark inside of the Mall of the Emirates.

We did not actually stop at The Frame, which is located in Zabeel Park, but it is so big, we were able to get a good view of it as we drove along. One of the main features of The Frame is the 93-meter long clear glass bridge with the transparent floor that connects the two 150-meter high vertical towers. It holds the title of "The Largest Frame in the World" and looking through it from one side you can see Old Dubai, and viewed through the other side, you can see modern Dubai, with all of its skyscrapers.

Ski Dubai was recognized as the "World's Best Indoor Ski Resort" in 2016 and 2017, and it claims to be the "World's

Largest Snow Park." Gomez took us to see this attraction, which, as stated previously, is actually inside the Mall of the Emirates. One thing Gomez pointed out as we drove into the parking garage was the amount of luxury cars like Rolls Royces and Bentleys, and sports cars like Maseratis and Lamborghinis that could be seen in this parking lot. He told us that it was not uncommon to see members of the Royal Family driving themselves around on the roads. He also pointed out that you could tell how important the driver of a vehicle was by the License Plates. If a plate had only a Single or Double-Digit number, you knew that person was pretty important, and the lower the number, the more important he was.

It was pretty cool (pardon the pun) and impressive seeing what looked like actual ski slopes, complete with lifts, behind this big viewing window you passed as you walked through the Mall. They even had an area below and off to the side of the slopes, where some penguins actually lived and played.

Burj Al Arab

The view from Jumeirah Beach, as shown below, or the drive-by view shown below, is about as close as you can get to Burj Al Arab, unless you have either a Room or a Dinner Reservation to get onto the property. It actually sits on its own private man-made island. This 5-Star (often called The World's Only 7-Star Hotel) exclusive Luxury Property is vigorously protected from unwanted guests, in the name of privacy for those who CAN afford to pay the tab to either stay or dine there.

I have to say though, that even from afar, this iconic symbol of Dubai, lives up to the hype, with its design resembling the sail of a Sailboat.

Fun facts about Burj Al Arab (per Gomez):
1) *Cheapest (1820 sq. ft.) rooms go for about $3000 USD/night*
2) *Most Expensive (8400 sq. ft.) rooms go for about $24,000 USD/night*

Bonus Fun Fact: Jumeirah means Beautiful when referring to Places or Things, whereas Jameela means Beautiful when referring to a Person.

After leaving Burj Al Arab, Gomez said there were two more main destinations he wanted to take us to. First of all, he wanted to take us out on the Palm Island - Palm Jumeirah – and past Atlantis. If you ever see any show or ad on TV about Dubai, they will almost surely show a view of the iconic Palm Jumeirah Island from the aerial view. This manmade "Eighth Wonder of the World" is the largest manmade island in the world! And it is quite an experience.

It is shaped like a Palm Tree with eight fronds branching out from the main stem on either side. As you drive to it up the main road from the Mainland, you are driving up the spine of the palm, if you will. And as you keep going toward the Atlantis Hotel, that is looming ahead of you in the distance, passing 10-15 story High-Rise condos on both sides of the road, all of a sudden, after having driven for a couple miles, you go down and UNDER the water through a tunnel for the last few hundred yards or so until you pop up on the surface by The Atlantis. If you've ever been to, or seen The Atlantis in The Bahamas, this one looks pretty much exactly like that one. At this point, we were now out in the Persian Gulf, about 3.6 kilometers from the Mainland! What a trip!!

We did not actually stop at The Atlantis. Gomez wanted to show us one of the views of the Mainland from out there, so we took the road past The Atlantis and went left for a mile or so until we reached Land's End. We turned there and went down a little further, until Gomez told the driver to pull over. We got out and were on a beach-like strip. Directly in front of us was Dubai's "Eye," their giant Ferris Wheel patterned after London's Eye, which, when completed, will be – you guessed it – the largest Ferris Wheel in the World, surpassing the current largest one, "The High Roller" which is in Las Vegas. Once again – everything is Bigger and Higher and Better in Dubai!

Another reason Gomez had brought us to our current location was to get a view of the skyscrapers over on the Mainland. And, just as he said, if you did not know better, you would think you were looking at the skyline of Manhattan in New York. We were viewing Dubai's Financial District, looking across the Persian Gulf.

After returning to the Mainland, Gomez said we were on our way to our final destination – Old Dubai and The Souks. As we drove along the highway on the way into Old Dubai, Gomez started telling us another story about some of the customs and culture over there. He turned around in his seat to ask Carol a question, and that's when we saw that Carol was nodding out, sitting straight up in her seat! I guess it's not surprising, when you recall that we had just come off an almost 15-hour Non-Stop flight and had been walking around on this tour for about five hours at this point. So, she had a right to be legitimately pooped!

Anyway, we all had a good laugh and he continued on with his story. It was really quite interesting. I'm not going to try and recount it here, but suffice to say, the serving (or not) of coffee to guests in the home is a very important ritual, and by the manner in which it is served and received, it can tell a lot about whether or not a guest is welcome or not.

As we drove through town and entered Old Dubai, we could immediately tell the difference. Old Dubai had regular-looking people and children out on the streets, going about their business. Some of the kids even had on school uniforms. This part of town just looked more "lived-in" and less "touristy/commercial" than the Downtown and Business Districts that we had just come from. We drove to the Abra Dock in Bur Dubai where we took the 10-minute Abra ride across the Dubai Creek.

The Souks

Once we were on that North side of the Creek, we were actually in Deira, which is where the Gold and Spice Souks are. The word "Souk" just means Marketplace or Bazaar, and the Spice and Gold Souks consisted of dozens, if not hundreds, of vendors displaying their wares in stalls lined up all along the lengths of this expansive shopping and looking area. In the old days, this used to be the meeting point for the Bedouins, but later it morphed into an area of trade and commerce for the vendors to ply their wares.

We stopped at one of the Spice Souks and Gomez explained some of the medicinal qualities of the various spices that were there. Then we strolled on down the street for a few blocks, marveling at all of the sights and smells that we were encountering. We had picked up our pace a bit, because the time was quickly approaching when we would have to turn around and head back to the airport so we wouldn't miss our flight.

We stuck our heads in a couple of shops featuring Gold and wound up at the end of the Souk dead-ending into a major street called Al Naif Road. Gomez asked us to be seated at a table at a small restaurant called the Naif Market. He ordered a couple of chicken Shawarmas for us and we hungrily gobbled them down. This consisted of chicken sliced off of a slab (like lamb off the slab for gyros) and wrapped in a burrito-like tortilla. The fries that came with it were actually inside the wrap, so that was different. It was good to get at least a little taste of the local foods, and since we were in a hurry by now, the choice was perfect.

Our driver had driven over to the Deira side of Dubai Creek, so when we were done eating, we made the 10-minute walk over to where he was, jumped in the car and headed to the airport. It was only about a 15-minute drive to the airport, and Gomez said that we were very lucky, because normally at that time on a Thursday evening, the rush-hour traffic would have extended into this time, but again, luckily it did not.

We said our goodbyes to Gomez at the airport, thanking him for a memorable six hours, and just like that, we were back on our own, and headed to Singapore!

VIII
SINGAPORE... AT LAST!

Before I actually get into some of the details and the places we visited and experienced in both Singapore and Indonesia on our trip, and of the great Family time we had, I'd just like to share a quick overview to recap what we learned about Singapore, in a high-level overview

After experiencing Singapore for nine days, the two words that sum up Singapore best are CLEAN and GREEN. A third word would be SHOPPING!

Singapore is Sooo clean. I imagine that is partially because of the strict laws and heavy fines they have for things like littering, spitting on the sidewalk, or chewing gum. *(Note: After having been back home for about 6 months, my wife remarked to me one evening that she had not even purchased any gum since we returned)* You may have heard rumors of some of these items, but let me tell you, they are true. We noticed that in some of the train stations, they don't even have trash cans, because littering is so discouraged, and people take it so seriously. Also, as we walked around the city and rode the train and bus, it seems like you would always see either someone sweeping up a few leaves on an already pristine street or pruning some branches over the roadside on some trees. And that brings me to that second word – GREEN.

Singapore is so lush and green. If you look on a globe of the world, you will see that it is just above the equator, 85 miles from it to be exact. So, the fact that it looks like you are in a tropical rainforest setting (if you discount the thousands of Public Housing (not low rent) High-Rise towers all over the city), should not come as a surprise. It also rained at least a little bit almost every day we were over there, although we were told that we must have brought the rain with us from Texas, as the few weeks before had been hot and dry. It was still in the 80's during the daytime, but it was just a little wet.

Now let's talk about Shopping. Wow! I have never been in any city with more Shopping Malls and/or Markets/Bazaars, etc. than Singapore. My niece, with whom we stayed, said there are over 300 malls in Singapore. When you Google "shopping malls in Singapore," it comes back with lists of over 100. Either way, this is Crazy Crack for a Shopaholic! One of the main shopping areas, Orchard Road, is a big boulevard lined on both sides for 2.2 kilometers (about 1.3 miles) with Malls. You can actually go underground and there is a street/walkway by which you can get to ALL of the stores. Some of these malls go up to 8-levels, including the underground levels. All of the top-name designer stores for everything – shoes, purses, clothing, perfumes, and anything else you can think of, can be found in these Orchard Street malls, as well as in other malls throughout the country.

In the Little India section of the city, the Mustafa Center is like an indoor Market, consisting of two city blocks worth of stalls, booths, and little shops housed under the roofs of two large 2-story buildings, each being 1-city block wide. Mustafa Center is where some of the cheapest prices can be found on a whole range of items. You can barter with the merchants here, but the prices are already so cheap, I did not even bother haggling. The US Dollar goes a long way in Singapore!

Now back to our story!!!

IX
A FAMILY REUNION

Remember, the reason we were journeying to Singapore in the first place was to reunite with and get to better know some of my Filipino family, who now live in Singapore.

We walked through Baggage Claim to get our bags and went through Customs with no problem. As we exited Customs and entered the area that led down to the waiting area, I almost instantly saw my niece Raech, her husband Bert and their 5-year old son Yuan – my Grandnephew - positioned almost directly in front of us about 50 yards away! I was pushing the cart with our four pieces of luggage, but Carol started sprinting toward them and everybody started yelling. We were finally in Singapore!

This reminded me of a scene, maybe 20 years or so earlier, when I arrived at the Manila airport and met my late Brother for the first time. The main difference was, that on that occasion, there was a whole lot of tears and crying going on, as the first two offspring of my Dad laid eyes and hands on each other for the first time.

But on this happy occasion, there were no tears, but multiple ear-to-ear smiling faces. After all the greetings and hugs, we went out to the large van they had called for, and piled in for the 45-minute or so ride to their condo.

Upon arrival and taking the elevator up to the 3rd floor of the 15-story building, we met "Ces" for the 1st time. Ces was short for Princess, and she was Raech and Bert's live-in housekeeper/cook/nanny. As we would find out during the trip, Raech and Bert pretty much depended on her for everything, including the care and feeding (literally) of their 5-year-old son Yuan. This tiny, slight-of-build young woman had been with the family since he was six months old, so she had been an integral part of raising him to this point. Raech called her a "Ninja" because she could fit into some of the same small spaces that Yuan could!

It was about 10am when we reached the condo in an area in Northern Singapore called the Woodlands, so we ate the breakfast that Ces had waiting on us and then crashed for a few hours before we would get up and begin the packed slate of outings and events that Raech had arranged for us for the next nine days.

When we got up and showered and left the condo for our 1st outing that evening, we immediately started getting a feel for Singapore, We walked the two or three blocks over to the closest MRT (Mass Rapid Transit) station, and on that short walk, we got our first taste of how clean – and humid – Singapore was. We also got an idea of the amount and size of the malls in Singapore. This MRT station gave direct access into a huge 7-level mall, the Causeway Point Mall. We later learned that most of the MRT stations around Singapore had direct access to malls, because they wanted to make it convenient for the residents in each area to shop. We also learned that this particular mall, with its 250+ stores, was the 7th largest suburban mall in Singapore. Additionally, we learned that the mall was named after the Causeway (bridge) that it was adjacent to. This Causeway connected the city of Woodlands, where Raech lived, to Malaysia, so we really WERE on the Northern border of Singapore, connected to the city of Johor Bahru in Malaysia by that bridge. It was the first land link ever constructed to link the two countries. When Singapore separated from Malaysia and got their independence in 1965, immigration checkpoints were added on both sides of the bridge. In hindsight, if I had known we were that close, I would have asked Raech to take us across the bridge to Malaysia, just so I could check off another country that I had been in! Oh Well. Maybe next trip!

    Carol and I were pretty zonked out from all the travel of the last couple of days by mid-evening, so we ALL just ate at a Chinese restaurant in the mall and headed back to Raech's home to rest up a bit. But before we went to bed, we actually started the process of getting to know my niece and her family and Singapore a little more intimately. Raech and Bert shared info with us on how the housing situation worked in Singapore, and told us how much their condo cost (in US Dollars) to give us some idea of how much it cost the average person to live in Singapore. I should say the average "foreigner" since she and Bert are from the Philippines and thus had to pay the "foreign rate" for housing. The government does offer 99-year leases to foreigners as their primary purchase option.

Their condo was a three-bedroom, two bath, 1200 square foot unit and cost them about $420,000 US Dollars. This was significantly more than I paid for my 3500 square foot, 4-bedroom, 2.5 bath, 2-car garage home with a swimming pool in the Dallas, Texas area!

One of the more interesting things that I took away from the evening's conversation was learning about the "forced integration" concept that was used in all the Housing Developments that were run by the state. In each development, it was mandated that there could only be a maximum of X% of a particular Nationality in each one. For instance, you might have a mix of maybe 50% native Singaporians, 10% Filipino, 15% Malaysian, 10% Indian, 10% Chinese, and maybe 5% other. The idea was that they did not want to have an over accumulation of one Nationality in one development to try and protect against Nationalism or maybe one-Nationality ghettos. Raech had mixed feelings about this. I am still not sure what I think of the idea and will have to give it more thought before I can come to any conclusions. But it seems like, for the most part, it works... at least, in Singapore!

Anyhow, after a couple hours of getting versed in Singapore housing, we finally took leave to our bedroom and both crashed like a ton of bricks!

Fun Fact About Singapore: If it were in the United States, it would be the 2nd most populated city, behind New York City. As of the 2017 estimates, NYC had about 8.6 million and Singapore had about 5.6 million folks.

X
FIRST FULL DAY

This was the day when we would start feeling like Tourists! Raech had packed a bunch of things for us to do into this first Weekend day in Singapore. She had chosen things that she and Bert and Yuan and Ces could also enjoy, since Bert would have to work next week during some of the weekdays. They had both taken a couple days later in the week off, as my two nephews would be joining us from the Philippines on next Thursday, my birthday.

We walked to the bus stop, which was right in front of Raech's building, and hopped on for the two-block ride to the MRT, the same MRT we had walked to last night. We quickly got a couple more lessons and insight about Singapore. Bert told us that the buses ran each route every eight minutes on weekends and every three minutes on weekdays, so you never had to wait very long for a bus. Also, after we got on the bus and were all seated and the bus started rolling, Bert immediately got up and offered his seat to an elderly gentleman. This was not just good manners, it was expected. There were even signs/pictures on the bus walls that said you must stand for the Elderly, Handicapped Persons, and Pregnant

Women. It seemed like Singapore really made a point of taking care of its citizens!

When we got to the MRT station and boarded our train for the 45-minute ride to our destination, Raech gave me a little more insight about the MRT system. The Singapore MRT system was similar to the one in Paris and it was very easy to get around on it if you knew the starting and exit stations and the endpoints of the direction you wanted to travel in. Raech also said that you could tell whether you were in the Singapore "suburbs" or the "city" by what elevation the train was at. If it was above ground, you were in the "suburbs," whereas whenever it went underground, you were in the "city."

The Merlion

At the end of our MRT journey, we reached our destination - Marina Bay. This is where the iconic Merlion is situated in Merlion Park at the mouth of the Singapore River. The Merlion is a statue with the head of a Lion and the body of a fish, thus the name Merlion is derived from Mermaid and Lion. It is the symbol of Singapore, as we would later learn, and pictures or representations of the Merlion are all over Singapore, from the huge Merlion statue on Sentosa Island, to the covers of boxes of chocolate, such as the ones we brought home.

The Merlion was pretty cool. After spending a few minutes admiring him and taking the obligatory picture of "Drinking the Water Spouting from the Mouth," we moved on to the next attraction we would be checking out, Gardens by The Bay.

Gardens by The Bay

Gardens by the Bay is one of the most popular tourist attractions in Singapore. It consists of three main attractions – the Flower Dome, the Cloud Forest, and the Supertree Grove. The Flower Dome and the Cloud Forest are basically like giant greenhouses on steroids with an attitude!

The Flower Dome

The Flower Dome is actually the world's largest columnless greenhouse. It is about three acres and had thousands and thousands of plants of all different varieties. The

Flower Dome consists of three levels and included an elevator you could take up to the top level.

It also had a Wizard of Oz theme going on among some of the exhibits and we passed The Scarecrow, The Tin Woodman, The Wizard, and his Hot-Air Balloon, interspersed among some of the sunflower fields on the main floor.

The Scarecrow and The Tin Woodman

Actually, in the Flower Dome is where we had the first instance of what would become somewhat of a recurring theme during our trip. As we were walking around on the ground level, I noticed this elderly, refined-looking Asian woman kind of staring at us, but I didn't think too much of it. I just figured that she had probably not seen too many Black people in her life, so she was staring. This happens from time to time, as you travel, depending on where you are. But about an hour or so later, I saw her again when we were upstairs by the cactus section. This time she could not help herself. She walked over to us, and started pointing at Carol's hair, and making the sign like she wanted to take a photo with her. So now we knew. It was the hair, not us! She was a nice enough lady, so Carol obliged her, and she nodded her thanks and went on her way. But again, this proved to be the beginning of a trend or theme, throughout our trip.

Cloud Forest

The Cloud Forest was a smaller dome overall, but it was taller than the Flower Dome. It had to be, because it housed a 115' tall waterfall, and had an artificial 138' Cloud Mountain built inside of it. The whole idea of the Cloud Forest was to replicate the cool moist conditions found in some of the tropical mountain regions in Southeast Asia and South America. It definitely gave the feel of being in a rain forest, with that waterfall, and the cool, misty air that emanated from it. It was pretty cool (pun intended).

By the time we got done with the Flower Dome and the Cloud Forest, we had walked and worked up quite an appetite. Fortunately for us, the next stop on Raech's exquisitely prepared itinerary was a place called Satay by the Bay.

Satay by the Bay

This was a giant "Hawker Centre" that was just a few hundred yards or so away from the domes. Now what a "Hawker Centre" was in Singapore was actually what we call a Food Court in the United States. There were dozens of food stalls all clustered in one area. This particular one was one of the main ones in Singapore. There was an ample variety of Malaysian, Singaporean, Indian, and other Asian cuisine to try and the prices were really cheap, especially considering this was in a major tourist area. Since the name of the place was Satay by the Bay, we decided to go with the Satay. There were guys in front of each Satay stand "hawking" their products. "Satay Heah, Satay Heah!" they yelled. It kind of reminded me of the Beer vendors at Major League baseball games yelling "Beer Here, Get your Ice-cold Beer!"

The Satay turned out to be a good choice. For those of you who may not know what Satay is, it's basically meat on a stick. We ordered some platters that had five different types of Satay on them – Pork, Chicken, Beef, Prawn, and Pork Bellies. I had never tasted Prawn or Pork Belly Satay before, but they were actually quite good. We ordered some Sugar Cane Juice and some Bandung, which is a Malaysian concoction made from rose petals, to wash the Satay down, and both were very tasty as well… and nice and cold!

Supertrees Grove

After finishing our meal, our next stop was the Supertree Grove, which was also relatively close, as it was part of the Gardens by the Bay complex. The Supertree Grove was definitely the highlight of the day – at least for me. I know that Carol really enjoyed the Flower Dome, with all of its different kinds of bright, pretty flowers. She had remarked that she thought the Monet Gardens, outside of Paris, which we had visited last year, were very pretty, but she said the Flower Dome was equally as beautiful, if not more so. And it definitely had a ton more varieties of flowers – from all over the world – than did the Monet Gardens.

But for me, you can only take so many flowers before they all start looking the same. So, when we got to the Supertrees and saw those impressive structures towering over us, that was more my speed. Each tree was about the height of a 16-story building, so they were pretty tall.

It was mid-evening when we got over to the Grove, and so the grounds were already packed, as people had come for the Light Shows that happened twice each evening, at 7:45 and

8:45. These shows were a coordinated light and music show known as the Garden Rhapsody. This is definitely a "must see" when visiting Singapore. We caught the last five minutes or so of the first show, and then just went to hang out and wait for the time to come for us to go up to the OCBC Skyway. Raech had purchased tickets for me and Carol to go on this adventure. What it was, was an elevated walkway that connected two of the larger Supertrees. When you were up there, it gave a great aerial, panoramic view of the entirety of Gardens by the Bay. Our entry time was a little over an hour away and that turned out to be perfect, as we got to see the 8:45 production of the Garden Rhapsody while we were waiting, and it was very nice. The music would play, and the various trees would flash on and off in all sorts of bright colors in rhythm with the music. The night we were there, the Trees were choreographed to the song "Oh What a Night." It was truly a spectacular scene to see and hear.

Pictures don't do it justice, but here are a couple of the trees in action.

First Full Day

The bottom photo above actually shows the two trees that are connected by the OCBC Skyway.

Once we got in line, it was about a 45-minute wait to get to the entry. It took so long because the elevator to the top only held about maybe 12-15 people. When we got to the top, it was worth the wait though. There were great views of the Financial District on the river, Singapore's version of the Eye Ferris Wheel, the Domes, and the other Supertrees.

While all of those sights were quite impressive, one of the more memorable things about being on the Skywalk was that queasy feeling you get in your groin (or at least I get it in mine) when you're at altitude with a sense of danger. That walkway was pretty darn narrow, and it was shaking and blowing in the wind quite a bit while we were up there. We wanted to take our time and see all the sights, but by the same token, we could not WAIT to get to that second tower and a sturdy platform back to relative safety!

After our aerial adventure on the Skywalk, Carol and I descended to the ground and took a taxi back home. Bert and Raech had told us where to catch one, as they had gone on home as soon as we got in the Skywalk line, as they had been up there before, and it was NOT free.

We took the 30-minute drive back home, and I did not realize how worn out I was until we got in the elevator to go to the 3rd floor, and actually almost stumbled into the living room when Raech opened the door. One Tiger Beer and Chili Crab snack later, and we were both out like a light!

XI
SUNDAY IS FUNDAY!

Sunday was going to be a shopping day… or at least, a shopping MALL day. Raech had plans for us to go to Orchard Road and then wind up the day down at Marina Bay to check out the Laser Light show.

Orchard Road

Orchard Road is a 2.2-kilometer (about 1.3 miles) section of a boulevard that has been turned into a retail and dining paradise, with over 5000 establishments in that relatively small area. It can accommodate so many stores and such because it starts and can be accessed underground, and some of the Anchor stores, such as ION Orchard, stretch eight levels high from basement to the top! It would literally take weeks to check out everything on Orchard Road, but Raech wanted to give us at least the Whirlwind Tour! Carol and I had to continually remind her that we are Old, and she needed to slow the pace down a bit. We actually did trim about five or six activities that she had planned for us during the course of our stay there. If we hadn't, they would have had to ship us back to the States in pine boxes – Cause of Death: Tour Excursion Overload!

The MRT actually pulled into the Orchard MRT station that gave you direct access to the ION Orchard mall. There were two main entrances into the mall at Level 1.

As we found out as we walked around, there were four underground levels beneath us, at underground levels, and there were four levels, starting at Level 1, above ground. When you go out onto Orchard Road and look at ION from the outside, it looks kind of futuristic, almost like a spaceship.

To say that ION Orchard was huge, would be a vast understatement. There were over 300 stores in the mall, including just about every High-End Fashion Store in the world. I was told that Halle Berry shops at the Harry Winston here. My wife and I ventured into the Kate Spade, which was on the first level, and the cheapest purse we saw was about $4000 US Dollars!

We window-shopped at a few more of the Luxury stores on the upper levels, then decided to go down to the underground levels, where the prices were said to be a little more affordable and for regular folks like us. The contrast was stark when we got to sub-Level 1. There were thousands of folks down there and it looked like and had the feel of a giant Flea Market atmosphere. As we walked down the main center corridor, we could peek over the rails and see some of the shops at the lower levels and they were also jam-packed. It looked like this corridor may have stretched underground for almost the whole length of Orchard Road, so we circled back toward where we went down, to go back up and outside using the ION Orchard exit.

Changing of the Guard

As we started walking down the street, we saw street performers doing their thing. The first one we came to was a little old man who kind of looked like he should have been a monk. He was rail-thin and had on a red basketball jersey with matching red sneakers. His thing was, spinning big strands of what looked like miniature coconut shells around his neck. All in all, it made for a very festive atmosphere as you sauntered down the street.

As far as we could see on both sides of the street, in front of us and behind us, were more and more malls. But remember, there was supposed to be over two kilometers worth of street filled with malls, and obviously, they were not kidding!

As we continued to walk, we suddenly heard the blare of some horns and the snare of drums. We looked up the street behind us and were pleasantly surprised to see a colorful marching band with three units approaching us as they marched crisply in cadence up the middle of the street. The first unit consisted of about 16 soldiers in their crisp olive-green uniforms, white helmets and combat boots laced with white strings. These guys were obviously part of a Drill Team unit, as they were doing maneuvers with their rifles, even as they continually marched forward.

The middle unit consisted of the band, a full complement of brass and drums such as you would find in any college football stadium in America during the Halftime show. These guys were sharp as well, in what looked to be their Dress uniforms, consisting of dark blue pants with a bold red stripe down each leg, a formal dinner-jacket type top, and topped with their bright red formal military caps.

The final unit consisted of about 20 guys dressed identical in uniform to the 2nd unit, but they also were marching with semi-automatic rifles held firmly against their right shoulders as they high-stepped forward.

We heard someone in the crowd say that this was the beginning of the Changing of the Guard Ceremony and the full ceremony would take place about a couple hundred yards in front of us, in front of what was, unbeknownst to us at that time, Singapore's version of The White House. We later learned that it was called the Istana.

Sure enough, as they kept marching, we saw them make a right-turn onto the Presidential grounds a little ways in front of us. Carol and I hurriedly picked up our pace and ran up the street so we could get in position to get a good view and get some good photos.

We watched and videotaped the entire ceremony, and it was pretty cool. It must have lasted about a half hour or so, during which time, the existing Guard marched out from behind the gates of the Presidential grounds, and the Replacement Guard, which were the ones we had seen marching in, replaced them during a ceremony filled with much pomp and circumstance and more rifle drill maneuvers.

Having been on the Drill Team while on my training base in the U.S. Air Force many years ago, I had a special appreciation for their handling of the rifles. Another thing that impressed me was how young these guys looked. When we got up close and personal with them after the ceremony, most of them looked like they were in their late teens or early twenties.

Sunday is Funday!

We also found out when we got back home after leaving Singapore, that we were very fortunate to catch this ceremony. They only do it once a month, on the First Sundays, starting at 5:45pm. So, our timing to luck up on this bonus treat was great!

Spectra Light Show

Our next stop in this full day that Raech had planned for us, took us down by the Marina Bay Sands hotel to watch the Spectra Light Show, which is a fantastic 15-minute choreographed Light and Laser show. We watched it from the grounds in front of the Sands, with the many skyscrapers of the Business District in downtown Singapore, serving as the backdrop across the Bay.

It was a truly spectacular show.

Marina Bay Sands Observation Deck

As you can probably tell from what I have laid out so far, this had been a very long day for us. But my niecy had been bound and determined to squeeze every bit out of her "tourist hosting handbag" and she had one more thing planned for us that evening – The Marina Bay Sands Skypark Observation Deck. But before I tell you about the Observation Deck, let me tell you a little bit about the Marina Bay Sands Hotel itself.

The Marina Bay Sands is one of those iconic representations of Singapore. If you ever see a travel advertisement or anything about Singapore, one of the things that I am sure you will see is what looks like a Cruise Ship perched on top of three giant, wide stilts or something. That is the Marina Bay Sands! It is 57 stories tall and the three "stilts" are actually the three towers of the hotel. The hotel is the sixth most expensive building in the world, ahead of such structures as Burj Khalifa in Dubai, which is the tallest building in the world, and behind a couple of nuclear power plants in Japan, among others. The property includes the world's largest atrium casino, with 500 tables and 1600 slot machines, a mall, a museum, an indoor skating rink, two large theaters, and seven "celebrity chef" restaurants, among its offerings.

When we alighted from the elevator from Hotel Tower 3 to the Observation Deck on the 57th level, the first view we were greeted with was of the Supertree Grove.

This outstanding vantage point gave a view of the entire forest. We were also looking down at the two Gardens by the Bay enclosures that we had been in a couple of days prior. As we made our way around the periphery of the Observation deck, we saw some of the hotel guests dining at the restaurant, which could be entered from the deck by going up about a dozen or so steps to the entrance. A little further on, and around the corner, we got our first glimpse of the famed Infinity Pool. This 150-meter pool lays claim to the title as "the world's largest elevated body of water outdoors!" We saw a couple of guests lounging in their white robes in some of the beds that were actually attached to the inner edge of the pool, and we observed a couple more guests actually in it, looking as though they were about to fall off! Amazing stuff!

We took a bit more time to take in some more of the views of the City across the bay, and then we settled into a couple of seats at the bar and ordered some drinks. We actually had our first "Singapore Slings" in Singapore in that bar. We were told that these were just a poor imitation of the original Slings, which were actually developed by a bartender, Ngiam Toon Boon, in 1913 at the famous Raffles hotel in Singapore. When we heard that, we made note to make sure and visit Raffles before we left. But when we got back to the apartment and researched it, we found out that it was currently undergoing renovations and would not be available until a couple of months after we left. Rats! Oh well, no Raffles, but all in all, another great day in Singapore!

XII
MONTIGO RESORT ON BATAM ISLAND, INDONESIA

Well, today was the day when we would venture out entirely on our own and add a third country to our list for this trip. We were spending the next day-and-a-half on Batam Island in Indonesia at the Montigo Resort! When we were doing our planning before we left the States, Raech said that she and Bert had been over to a couple of the resorts in Indonesia and this was one of the ones that she recommended.

We had to take a taxi to get to the Ferry Terminal where we could catch our ferry. We had purchased the ferry tickets online before we left the States to make sure we could get the date and time we wanted. The taxi to the terminal took about 45 minutes, which was slightly more than the actual 40-minute ride on the ferry to the island.

We had to go through Immigrations and Customs, just as you do at an airport when visiting any foreign country, but this process went smoothly and quickly. No Visa is needed for a U.S. Citizen going from Singapore to Indonesia.

Interesting Fact about Indonesia: It has the third largest population in the world, behind only China and India.

One thing I noticed on the ferry trip across was how many freighters we saw parked all over the place between Singapore and Batam Island. A few months after returning to the States, we saw a travel program about Singapore, and we found out why there were so many of them. It turns out that Singapore is the world's second busiest port in terms of total shipping tonnage, and it ships about a fifth of the world's shipping containers!

So anyway, after a nice, easy ride over, we pulled into the dock at around 11:40am. As we disembarked and were walking down the pier, we caught a young girl who was going toward the ferries, trying to sneak and take a picture of Carol. After we busted her, she started laughing nervously and since she apparently did not speak any English, we kind of motioned and asked her if she wanted to take a picture with Carol.

Remember I told you earlier about that older Asian woman in Gardens by the Bay, who was fascinated with Carol's hair? Well, apparently this young lady was too! She wanted to touch the hair and then she was happy. There must be a real scarcity either of Black women, or of Black women with curly reddish-brown hair, around Singapore – LOL!

After about 10-15 minutes, they started loading us onto the bus that would take us to our resort, and after a short 10-

minute ride, we were there. The main reception/check-in desk was in a big open-air lobby, and as you stood in it and looked over to the left, you could see the Straits of Singapore, which was the body of water separating Singapore and Indonesia.

Interesting Fact about Batam Island: It is the closest part of Indonesia to Singapore, with the closest points being only 5.8km (about 3.5 miles) apart

They greeted us with a glass of some nice, refreshing ginger-type drink and a cool towel, as it was very humid. After we checked in, they said it would still be a couple of hours (3pm) before our room was ready, so they suggested that we ride with one of the staff in one of their little golf-cart like trams, to take a tour of the property. He took us down a couple of hills and around a couple of bends and we arrived at the restaurant area.

We did not need to go any further, as it was about 1pm by this time, so we were definitely ready for some chow!

Carol ordered some nice fresh coconut water while we waited.

By the time we finished lunch and got back to the lobby, our room was ready, so we caught another intra-property shuttle to our villa.

It was a nice-sized villa, with a kitchen, living room, bedroom, bath and shower, walk-in closet, and a balcony with a private Infinity pool and a lovely view of the Straits. Very nice!

Montigo Resort on Batam Island, Indonesia

An hour or so after we had gotten settled in, the phone rang, and it was the Front Desk asking us if we would be in the room in the next 50 minutes or so. We told them that Yes, we would be there, as we had not planned on going anywhere. About 30 minutes later, six staff members, including a guitarist, showed up at the front door with a huge slice of chocolate Birthday cake and an Indonesian rendition of Happy

Birthday. My Birthday was in three days, so I guess they had obtained that data from my registration. That was truly a nice surprise!

Shortly after the Birthday Gang left, it started raining and it rained throughout the entire evening. It's a good thing that we had planned on just having a nice quiet, relaxing time at the resort. We made ourselves comfortable in that big cozy bed and just chilled.

Interesting Story: One eventful thing came out of that evening. As we lay there, we started discussing the Children's book – Mia Goes to Jamaica – that I was working on, and Carol sketched on a piece of paper what her idea was for the Front Cover of that book. We poked and tweaked it a little, but basically, as soon as we returned to my niece's place the following evening, we had her scan that drawing in, and we e-mailed it off to our Illustrator in the Philippines, and that is how and where the cover of that book was born.

Even though it rained all night, the serenity and atmosphere and beauty that we gleaned from that short power-rejuvenation/recovery trip was just what we needed at that point in our trip to prepare us for the rest of the trip. We knew that Raech had tons more activities and sights and adventures planned; and my two nephews would be arriving in a couple of days – one, with his wife and toddler; so, we definitely were grateful for the opportunity to recharge on that island!

XIII
FAMILY TIME WITH THE GONZALS

We checked out of the resort at about Noon the next day and caught our ferry back to Singapore. The trip back was pretty uneventful until we got to the Customs and Immigration checkpoint in Singapore. I flashed my passport and papers and walked right on through, but when I turned to see where Carol was, it was happening again... her and that hair! She and the Customs lady at the checkpoint were engaged in some joyful conversation and once again, it revolved around that hair! Carol seemed to be really enjoying the conversation, and when she caught up with me, she said she still could not believe how all these women were so fascinated with her hair.

When we got outside the terminal, ready to get a cab to take us back to Raech's place, we realized that we had no idea what to do. Fortunately, there was another American at the Taxi Stand and he saw us looking all lost. He told me that I needed to download an app called GRAB (their version over there of Uber) to call cabs in the future, but he went ahead and called one for us this time. We were very appreciative.

The GRAB guy arrived in about 10 minutes or so, and it only took him about 30 minutes to get us back home. He was very friendly and chatty, and we learned quite a bit from him during the trip. He told us that Singapore consisted primarily of Malaysians, Chinese, and Indians and that it actually used to be a part of Malaysia. We did not know that.

Another thing that was reinforced with us on the drive home was how beautiful and lush and green and clean Singapore was. Carol remarked during that trip that it is one of the most naturally beautiful, if not THE most beautiful, places she has ever visited.

Once we got home that evening, our trip was seriously segueing from Tourist Time to Family Time. This was a great time to start learning more about my family, as other than the time when Raech and Bert had come to visit us when we lived in Arizona, and when Raech joined Carol and me in Bangkok on one of my work assignments over there, I had not really spent any time with my Filipino family.

Raech brought out her wedding album to show us, and let me tell you, Filipino weddings are quite elaborate and over the top –at least hers was, and she said it was typical. When we returned home and saw the movie, "Crazy, Rich, Asians" they also had an over-the-top wedding, so maybe it's a cultural thing?

Raech also brought out the Karaoke machine that had over 7000 songs in it in English and Mandarin. She brought out the Wine along with the machine, so before long, she and I and Bert and Carol and young Yuan were singing and dancing away.

Raech and I also had some quiet time alone that evening and she was able to tell me things about my brother, like how he had met and courted his wife and how THEIR song came to be Conway Twitty's "Hello Darling." Moments such as those we spent together that night were some of the most precious ones of the trip.

XIV
LITTLE INDIA AND
THE MUSTAFA MARKET

The rest of the family was supposed to arrive Wednesday evening, but Carol and I had a full day of exploring Singapore alone that day. That was to be our first day of really navigating the MRT system by ourselves. I felt pretty confident by this time though, because in addition to having already traveled on it a couple of days with Raech and Bert, Raech also told me to download an app called SG MRT, which had all the lines and stops on it. If you are ever in Singapore, I definitely recommend that you download this app. It is interactive, and if you touch the station you are at and your destination station, it will light up the path you need to get there, including any crossline trains you need to take. For instance, we knew our destination for that day, The Mustafa Market, was near the Farrer Park MRT. So, we punched in Woodlands North and Farrer Park, and it highlighted the path we would need to take from the Red Line to the Blue Line to the Purple Line, and it told us approximately how long the journey would take – 44 minutes.

Most of the people we had encountered on the MRT to this point had been pleasant enough, but on this particular trip, an elderly gent decided to strike up a conversation with us. He introduced himself and told us he was the retired assistant Superintendent of Police in Singapore, having retired 16 years ago at the age of 55. He was very informative, telling us that there were four languages spoken in Singapore (English, Malay, Indian, and Chinese), among other little nuggets. He also showed us what he said was the largest lake in Singapore, as the train passed it. He also said that there were no more racial problems in Singapore, and that everyone lived together in peaceful co-existence. All in all, this was a very nice conversation and made our ride to Mustafa Market even more enjoyable than it normally would have been.

Mustafa Market was huge. It is in the Little India section of Singapore and it consists of two 2-story buildings, each a full CITY BLOCK long, full of little shops and stores and stalls. It was basically a giant flea market under two roofs. Whereas Orchard Road, where we had been a few days earlier, had a lot of high-end stores, Mustafa Market was definitely the place to go for bargain basement deals where you could haggle with the merchants to get the prices even lower than they were. Some of the prices were already so low against the strong US Dollar, that I did not even bother haggling.

We loaded up on souvenirs to take back home at Mustafa. Among the gifts we purchased were some Battery Packs for mobile phones. These went for around $30 in the U.S. and we got them for about $14 – half price.

They had everything in Mustafa market, from luggage to electronics to clothing to grocery stores to pharmaceuticals.

We had a late lunch at one of the Indian Restaurants in Little India. We peeked into one that looked to be almost full, so we figured the food must be pretty good there, and gave it a shot. After eating, we spent a couple more hours walking around Little India, checking out some of the outdoor stalls in one area that were all under a huge tent, and then started making our way back to the MRT station to go home.

It was pouring down rain by this time, so I had to run across the street to a store and purchase an umbrella before we could continue on to the station. We boarded our train and got back to the Woodlands station and decided to check out their mall before heading back home. This was a 7-level mall, so it was no slouch. As Raech would tell us later, pretty much every residential section of the city had malls in their MRT stations to make it convenient for residents to spend their money! Sounds pretty smart to me! After looking around a bit, we ate dinner at the Hot Tomatos restaurant (best barbecued ribs I had in Singapore) and got back home at around 9:30pm.

Warren and Family Arrive

When we entered the apartment, we were lovingly greeted with hugs and smiles by my nephew Warren and his wife DhaDa and their 3-year old son JD (John Daniel), who had arrived from the Philippines shortly before we got home. My other nephew, Miko, who was also scheduled to arrive that evening from the P.I. had gotten delayed and would not be getting in until 3am.

So, after staying up chatting for a bit with Warren and his family, we crashed relatively early. Warren did make one suggestion before we went to bed, that I definitely intended to follow up on when we got back home. After hearing about my "Mia Goes to Jamaica" book, he suggested that we contact the Jamaican Tourism Bureau to see about getting it placed with them. I marked this down on our list of definite "To Do's" when we returned to the States!

XV
OCTOBER 11™
MY 64™ BIRTHDAY

We were awakened that morning by the whole family, including Apol, who had arrived overnight, serenading me with Happy Birthday, and holding a big old Birthday Cake.

Happy Birthday Serenade & Cake

When we put on our robes and joined everyone in the dining room, there was a giant "Happy Birthday Uncle Warren" banner hanging on the wall and balloons hanging from the ceiling all over the place. I truly felt special. They then sat us down to a breakfast comprised of U.S. and Philippines cuisine. Among the Filipino food was Noodles for Good Luck. They also had bacon and pancakes, but had never tried hot syrup on their pancakes, so we were able to turn them on to that, doing a kind of mini cultural exchange right there at breakfast!

We spent the rest of the morning talking and learning more about each other and sharing the family history. One kind of cool thing that came to light as Warren and I were talking was how it seemed like he and I had almost grown up similar in regard to the relationships we had with our fathers and the communities we grew up in.

We were both named Warren, the sons of two Warrens. Both of our fathers were highly respected in their local communities. His Dad (my Brother) had been a police inspector and community organizer, who had planned on running for local office before he was diagnosed with cancer. My Dad (his Grandfather) had also been well-respected in the community in his roles as Barber (where everyone came to discuss politics, just like in the movie Barber Shop) and as a Union Man at his job in a steel mill.

The common thread, and a gene I believe that all four of us Warrens shared was a desire to help the downtrodden. I had also been involved in community organizing and HAD run for City Council in my current community and Warren has served humanity by doing five years missionary work in South America, along with his wife, right after they got married.

I also found out a lot about Warren and Apol in regard to their professional and personal lives that morning. But I don't want to bore you guys with that, so back to our Touring!!

The Singapore Zoo

I really have to give credit to my niece, Raech. She did a great job of planning out the itinerary during our stay, in such a manner that Carol and I could go off on our own at the

October 11th My 64th Birthday

beginning of our stay, and then participate in all of the more family-oriented activities once the entire family arrived. I guess it makes sense to do that, but she did it in such a masterful fashion that, if she ever wants to retire from her job as a Purchasing Agent for Proctor & Gamble, she can definitely start a new career as a vacation Planner/Tour Guide ☺!!! Today's first activity, at the Singapore Zoo, was a perfect example of this.

You could tell this zoo was designed with families in mind, because as soon as you entered, the first building you saw was the Stroller rental place, where parents could rent strollers for their young kids. They also had a couple of trains/trams that went all throughout the premises and this was of great value to some of the patrons on the other end of the spectrum, the seniors.

This zoo had a great assortment of animals, reptiles, and birds. One of the first things you saw if you looked down into the water from the first bridge you crossed, was a huge Alligator. I don't know if I've ever seen one that large. At first, I thought it was just a fallen tree laying in the water.

There were many, many more animals to attract and keep our interest over the next two-three hours that we spent there. We saw pygmy hippos from a vantage point where we could actually see them swimming under water, with their heads above the water. There were Orangutans and other little monkeys of all types, elephants, lions, and tigers, but no bears. Oh my! The one tiger they had was a beautiful rare White Tiger. He and the one Lioness we saw sunning out in their natural habitats, looked as though they KNEW that this was their kingdom and that they ruled over it.

There was also a great marine show featuring a huge seal, performing all kinds of tricks as he slid on and around his stage and pond. The bottom couple of rows in that amphitheater had signs on them saying not to sit there if you didn't want to get wet, and shortly after the show started, we found out why. Mr. Seal would make quite the large splash as he slid into the water and performed some of his aqua feats.

All in all, it was a great way to spend a relaxing afternoon, even though we got a little rain dumped on us from the afternoon storm.

When we got done with the Zoo, we went out into the Plaza and had some dinner before partaking of the evening activity – the Night Safari. There were still a couple of hours to go before it got dark, so we had time. We spotted a Good Old KFC, and Carol and I were elated, as we were ready for some more American food by that time! Raech, Bert, and Yuan had already been to the Night Safari, so they headed on back home, and left the rest of us there, where we ate and chatted until it was time to go board the tram for the Night Safari.

Night Safari

The Night Safari, which opened in 1994, was the world's first nocturnal zoo and is one of the most popular tourist attractions in Singapore. It houses over 2500 animals set in an open-air zoo in a humid tropical forest, designed to closely simulate each specie's natural habitat. The lighting was also designed to simulate a full moon, so the animals would be further fooled into thinking it was nighttime. It was pretty cool.

You could either walk through it on one of the four trails that went throughout each of the seven regions it was divided into, or you could ride along in the comfort of the tram. We took the tram, which took about 35 minutes to complete its route. The only bad thing about this attraction was that, even though we had pre-purchased tickets, the line to actually get on the tram was about as long as the tram ride itself. We must have spent at least 30-40 minutes waiting in that line.

But once we finally got on, it was interesting seeing the animals doing what they normally do at night when no tourists are around. We saw Rhinos and Malaysian Tigers and Elephants and Giraffes and lots of different kinds of deer and many more creatures. Most of them were just chilling or clustered together in herds grazing. The way the park was designed, they were not even aware that we were passing through, as we were far enough away to be unobtrusive, even though we were close enough to get good views of them.

There are also a couple of shows that can be seen at Night Safari. We were not aware of them while we were in Singapore, but found out about them during post-trip research. There was a 7-minute fire-twirling and drum show called the Thumbuaka Performance that was offered right outside the entrance about four times a night, and there was a 25-minute show inside the ground of the Safari called "Creatures of the Night." In this show, the natural abilities of some of the most fascinating animals in the park – like hyenas and meerkats and otters and civets and binturongs are displayed. It definitely sounds like a very entertaining show

XVI
SENTOSA ISLAND

Wait a Minute! Before we go any further, let me ask you. "Are you tired yet?"

I know Carol and I were. We had been in Singapore for seven days now, and by the time we rolled out of bed on that Friday morning, we were Pooped, with a Capital P! Even as I write this, I can't believe how much we had seen and experienced and how pretty much non-stop we had been going since we arrived in Singapore. But there is a lot to do and take in over there, and since the reality is that we would probably never get back over to that part of the world, we wanted to experience as much as we could. After all, we wanted to have enough interesting experiences to share with you guys (smile)!

Raech and I actually had some more time to bond and share some family stories on the MRT ride over to Sentosa Island that morning. I wanted her to know as much about her Granddad (my Dad) as she could, so she could understand a little of her roots. That was a special time for the both of us.

We actually had an unexpected "adventure", or should I say, "misadventure" when we got off our MRT train to walk thru the station to change to the next train we had to catch. This was a huge station, and the eight of us were just kind of walking along single-file and leisurely. At one point, Carol looked back and asked Raech, where Yuan, her 5-year old son was. She looked around and did not see him, and he was not with Bert or any of the rest of us either. Panic quickly set in. Raech and Bert were used to having their young Nanny, Ces, along with them most times when they traveled, and Yuan usually hung with her. She was just 22 and had about as much energy as him. But they had sent her along earlier that morning to go and camp out and reserve one of the five Cabanas at Adventure Cove for us, so we would have a headquarters to branch out from once we arrived there.

All of us started yelling Yuan's name, and we split up and went in different directions to search for him. Bert went back the way we had come from, Raech found an official to tell her what was going on, Warren branched in another direction, and Carol and I stayed put, in case Yuan showed up back here. It was crazy! I had never seen such fear in anyone's eyes before. But any of you who have ever been separated from a young child before, can feel what she was going though, I'm sure.

Bert came back up the escalator we had originally ascended – empty-handed. About this time, Yuan suddenly appeared out of nowhere, smiling like all get-out. A big wave of relief swept over us all, but Raech just grabbed him and started shaking him like a rag doll, telling him he better not ever run off like that again! All of this took about maybe two or three minutes.

Oh well, on to Sentosa. It promised to be an interesting day!

Sentosa Island

Sentosa Island is said to be the most popular tourist attraction in Singapore. Let me briefly list some of its attractions:

1. Resorts World Singapore which includes the following:
    - Adventure Coves Waterpark
    - S.E.A. Aquarium
    - One of the 2 casinos in Singapore
    - Universal Studios
    - The Hard Rock Singapore
    - Royal Albatross Pirate Ship
    - Butterfly Park and Insect Kingdom
    - Madame Tussauds Singapore
    - Sentosa Luge and Skyride
    - Palawan Beach

We actually took one of the other attractions, The Singapore Cable Car, as our transportation to get over to the island. Each of the gondola cars had two seats, holding up to about six people total. It was about a 20-minute ride on the Mount Faber Line, boarding at the Harbourfront Station and then going up over the hills and jungle toward Mount Faber, before turning back around and going over the Harbor and onto Sentosa Island. The views of both Sentosa and the downtown city skyline were fantastic from up there. It gave us a great opportunity to kind of scope out the park, so we would have an idea of where everything was when we landed.

Sentosa Island

We disembarked from the cable car and headed on over toward the cabanas, which we had spotted from the air. Sure enough, as we approached our cabana, Cabana B, there was

Ces and her smiling face, greeting us as we approached. We had arrived at our headquarters for the day!

The cabanas were right in front of the giant wave pond, BluWater Bay, which was the centerpiece of the whole park, it seemed.

Each cabana had a changing area and a shower right behind the back curtain, so we quickly shed our outerwear, and were soon splashing and cavorting in BluWater, along with the rest of the Happy Guests.

After a trip down the Lazy River, throughout and around the whole circumference of the park it seemed, Carol and I regrouped back at the Cabana. After a brief respite, we got back on the main street to see where it would lead us. We ran into Dhada (Warren's wife) and Raech, and Carol went with them as they went into a section of the park called Splashworks. This was where they had a bunch of rope-climbing apparatus and balance-beams, where the penalty for falling out of each was –

you guessed it – making a huge splash as you fell into the water. I sat on a bench to watch them, waiting for the fun to come as they fell, but surprisingly enough, none of them hit the water even once. Rats! That was no fun (smile)!

We left there and right across the pathway from it was Rainbow Reef. This was a huge manmade reef that had over 20,000 fish in it, where you could go snorkeling to check them out. You could look into the tanks from the sidewalk as you passed them, and the fish were very colorful. We decided to go in. After you entered, you had to don a lifejacket and sit on a small platform immersed partially in the water as you waited for your group to be allowed in. Warren and Dhada went first, then Raech.

When it was time for me and Carol to go, something came over me when I stuck my head into the water for some reason and I could not go. Carol wanted to turn back with me, but I told her to go on and enjoy it without me, and she did. I guess I still had not mentally gotten over not being able to go into any water unless my feet could touch the bottom and this bottom was 10' deep.

By the time we left the Reef, we were pretty hungry. In honor of the State Fair of Texas, which was going on back in The States at that time, I got a Corn Dog and a Turkey Leg for Carol and me. They weren't as good as the ones in Texas ☹!

We spent the next couple of hours pretty much just chilling, occasionally getting in the wave pool. After a couple more photo ops, we decided to call it a day for Adventure Cove.

The group split up after we left the Park. Carol and I wanted to go back to Mustafa Center in Little India to take advantage of those low prices and pick up some more souvenirs for the folks back home.

After leaving Little India, we did have one more piece of excitement that was only fitting, to bookend how we had started the day with Yuan going missing for a few minutes.

After we had made two MRT exchanges and got on our final Red Line train back to the Woodlands, we had an unscheduled stop about three exits before ours and they made everyone get off and go to board the next train that was coming on our route. We never did find out what happened, but I guess you have to have a little weirdness from time to time on vacation, just to keep that edge on… Not!

When we got to our MRT exit, we decided to have a little dinner before going in, as it was around 10pm at this time, and we didn't know if the folks would still be up when we got home. Carol had some Roast Chicken and Fried Rice and String Beans from one of the vendors there, and she remarked that it was the best meal she had had since we got to Singapore – and it only cost $4.

XVII
OUR LAST FULL
DAY IN SINGAPORE

For some reason, our breakfast conversation that morning turned into a comparison of burial and wake customs between Filipino customs (remember, all of my nieces and nephews here were Filipino) and Jamaican customs. My wife Carol is Jamaican.

Carol told about the "setup" that Jamaicans have, which is done the night before the funeral services and burial. Setup is basically like a big party/celebration that is given by the family, whereby a band is hired, and the entire community is invited, and they just eat and sing and dance and celebrate the memory of the Dearly Departed all through the night. Carol also told of how they usually don't bury their dead immediately, waiting for sometimes as long as two weeks to allow family members that live abroad to come back.

Raech explained that the Filipino custom is to bury within three days if possible, but that they also will push that date back if there are family members overseas. She also said that some people are buried in multi-level crypts, and some of the crypts even contain kitchens, so that food can be prepared right in the crypt and put on the altar as an offering during the Dia de Los Muertos (Day of the Dead) ceremonies. This tradition came down to the Philippines from Spain, since the Philippines was under Spanish rule and occupation for over 300 years.

Very interesting conversation…

This was our last full day in Singapore and Raech had a full slate of activities lined up for us. We would be going back to Sentosa Island. This time, our main attraction was the S.E.A. Aquarium, followed by a quick stop in the Casino.

We actually got to the Island by monorail instead of cable car this time. We boarded the Sentosa Express line from the 3rd level of the Vivo City Mall and it was a quick 3-minute ride from there over to the Island.

S.E.A. Aquarium

Upon entering the S.E.A. (South East Asia) Aquarium, you walked into a big atrium area with one narrow corridor branching off to the right and a larger one going to the left. The one to the right, with a blue light coming from it, seemed more interesting, so that's the way we went.

That hallway turned out to be pretty cool, as it was a long corridor with a curved ceiling in which you were walking under a huge tank filled with all sizes and types of fish. Among these were a hammerhead shark and another large shark that we noticed immediately upon entering. The tank also extended down on both sides of us as we were walking along.

It reminded me of a tank on the property of The Atlantis Resort in Nassau, Bahamas.

The aquarium was designed kind of like a maze in the way it directed your path as you walked along. As we moved forward and around the bend in one direction, we could look to the right, and see some folks moving in another direction on a level below us. There were plenty of colorful animals and large species including, the aforementioned sharks, and groupers and manta rays, etc.. I guess they were so colorful because a lot of them were from various reefs around the world. We found out from the literature that we received that there were over 100,000 actual marine animals in there from over 1000 species. Here is a look at a few of them.

Moray Eel

School of Jellyfish

One of the claims to fame for this aquarium was that it boasted "The World's Largest Aquarium Viewing Panel." It was "ginormous" to use a word from my granddaughter. It was situated in what appeared to be approximately the middle of the whole aquarium and it was so large that it was set in a theater, much like what you would see when you enter a typical multiplex theater in The United States or any major city these days.

There were about three or four rows of chairs up front, and then after going up a couple of steps there were maybe a half dozen or so more rows. As this was about the mid-way point in the aquarium, folks were camped out here in chairs, at some of the round tables they had in there, or just seated on the floor, either checking out the view in front of them, or else just chilling, relaxing, or taking the time to get a snack. There was a snack bar located conveniently at the back of this room.

The Casino

We walked around for maybe another hour or so taking in all the aquarium had to offer and then took our leave, exiting back out onto the Resorts Sentosa property, of which this was a part. We came to a sign on the grounds that sort of gave us some direction, and we headed off toward The Casino.

Now my wife knows I like to gamble, so I told her we would spend no more than an hour in the casino – win, lose, or draw. She accepted these terms, and in we went! I really just wanted to check it out, and it was actually pretty small compared to Vegas Casinos, of course, and even compared to some of the ones that I had been to on Indian Reservations back in Arizona and Oklahoma. But it was one of only two casinos in Singapore, so if you wanted to try your luck, there weren't a whole lot of different venues to choose from.

A little before the one hour-mark was up, I ran out of the money that I had brought in to gamble with, but I figured since we still had a little time left, I'd hit the ATM machine and grab just a wee bit more to give the tables one last try. But as I walked around and around looking for one, I couldn't locate any. I asked one of the officials there, and they said there were no ATM's inside the casino. If you wanted one, you would have to leave the premises. I took this as a sign, and rounded up Carol, close to the slots that I had left her at. She had exhausted her casino allowance as well, so we quietly walked out of that place with our tails between our legs (sigh…).

VivoCity Mall –Largest in Singapore

Since Raech and Warren and the gang had gone on ahead after we all left the Aquarium, Carol and I were on our own again. We caught the Sentosa Express monorail back over to the HarbourFront MRT Station to begin our journey homeward. But since the monorail let us out right on the 3rd level of VivoCity, which is the largest mall in Singapore, with five levels (three above-ground and two basement levels) and

340 stores, so we decided that we might as well check it out while we were right there, as this would be our last chance.

It was definitely huge, with a number of high-end stores, as well as some of the typical types of stores you would see in any average mall in the States. But after walking around for a little over an hour, and having seen maybe one third or so of one level, we decided that that was enough, so we went on to the MRT and caught our Yellow Line train to start us on our way home.

When we got to the Woodlands MRT, where Carol had purchased dinner the previous night, we decided to get a couple of dinners to go from that same Hawker Stand. Carol had one more instance there regarding her hair, when the woman behind the counter selling the food, motioned as to how pretty her hair was. She was used to it by now, so she just smiled and thanked her.

Warren and Family Leave

By the time we walked into the apartment, it was almost 11pm, and we got there just in time to see Warren and his family off, as they had a late flight back to the Philippines that night. So, we said our goodbyes to them, and exchanged hugs and kisses, and retired for the night, in what would be our last night in Singapore.

XVIII
SUNDAY, OCTOBER 14TH
THE JOURNEY IS OVER

Our flight was not scheduled to leave that night till around 9pm, so we were able to sleep in, getting up at around Noon, and have a lazy day. Bert and Raech prepared a nice lunch for us, as Ces, the housekeeper/nanny/cook was off on Sundays.

So, after lunch, we basically just chilled and started exchanging more "getting-to-know-you" stories, having some more quality family time. Late that afternoon, we called GRAB and our driver arrived about 5pm. We said our goodbyes to the family with a lot of appreciation and thankfulness for all they had done to make us welcome over the last 9 days. This really HAD been a special trip with the family bonding combined with the tourist part!

The GRAB driver was a 50-year old Singaporean named Alfie, and he made the 30-minute drive to Changi Airport very entertaining, with his outgoing personality. Along the way, he pointed out various things to us as we drove past them, like the Army base that housed the Chinook and Apache Helicopters in their arsenal. He told us they also had F-15 and F-18 fighter jets. This struck a chord with me as I had worked with the F-15's when I was in the US Air Force back in the late '70's, stationed in Germany.

Alfie also pointed out to us, a new mall on the airport grounds that had just opened a couple of days ago. This was the new 10-story Jewel Changi Airport mall, which had been built on the site of the airport's old Terminal 1. This mall was supposed to give the Orchard Road Shopping area a run for its money. If we ever DO return to Singapore, we will definitely have to put this on our list of MUST-SEE places to visit before leaving town.

Upon arrival at the airport, I must say that the check-in process was one of the smoothest and fastest that I have ever experienced. There were dozens of futuristic-looking kiosks all over the place. Within seconds of us getting into the area, an Emirates representative approached us and directed us to the Baggage Drop area, where another gentleman directed us to the scales, where we weighed and checked our bags.

Then we quickly went through two more checkpoints, presenting our Boarding Passes and Passports, and Voila! We were inside the Passenger/Shopping area. It was actually quite lovely and impressive. We saw a shop with some Singapore sweatshirts, and since that was exactly what our daughter had asked for, we were able to use the last of our Singapore dollars on these, getting some very nice sweatshirts in a 3-for-2 deal.

I could not believe our trip was almost over. We still had about two hours to go before boarding, so we settled in for the wait, and I broke out my notebook to begin recording that day's activities while they were still fresh in my mind.

Note: One tip I want to leave you with is, if you are departing from the C gates at Terminal 1, get any food and snacks you want to munch on, BEFORE taking the moving sidewalks to the gate area. I found this out the hard way, when Carol and I got a little hungry and I had to take that almost 15-minute each way back to the area where all the food vendors were set up. Just a word to the wise!

Well, that's about it. The rest of the trip and the flights home were pretty uneventful. We left Singapore around 9pm that Sunday night and arrived in Dubai at about 1am Local time. The plane, an Airbus A380, was so empty that pretty much everyone on it was able to stretch out in the 3-across rows to get some good rest/sleep. The only excitement on that flight occurred when the flight attendants had to usher a very drunk woman to her seat!

After about a 2-hour layover in Dubai, we boarded our flight back to Dallas, and we got in right on schedule at almost 10am Monday, Local time, after a 16-hour flight.

I hope you enjoyed my recounting of some of our adventures and experiences in Dubai and Singapore during this more-than-likely, once-in-a-lifetime trip for us. For those of you who have ever had the pleasure of getting to know long-lost or never-known relatives, hopefully this book rang true to some of the emotions and such that are encountered when going through such joyous times. Hopefully, My Dad is looking down on us, smiling and knowing that two branches of his lineage have been reconnected, and can march forward together in time, each knowing a little more about the root that they sprang from and about each other.

While this was a Travel story and guide, it was much, much more than this to me and I am grateful and thankful to The Lord for allowing us to reconnect and strengthen the family bonds that we share.

...But It's Not the End

We were blessed with one more treat on the flight home form Dubai to Dallas. As we crossed over the North Pole at around 4:20 am, I awakened and was greeted with a majestic view of the sunrise over the curving earth globe. It was a wonderful reminder of how beautiful this planet that God created for us really is. Although a photo cannot do justice to that view, I am providing one here anyway.

APPENDIX A

How Singapore Compares to Select U.S. and World Cities in Population and Area as of 2017/2018

City	Population	Area (sq.mi.)
Mumbai	*12,478,447*	*233.0*
London (2018)	9,126,366	607.0
New York (2017)	8,622,698	468.4
Bangkok (2010)	*8,305,218*	*605.7*
Singapore (2018)	**5,638,700**	**279.0**
Los Angeles (2017)	3,999,759	502.8
Rome (2018)	*2,857,046*	*496.3*
Chicago (2017)	2,716,450	227.3
Houston (2017)	2,312,717	637.5
Paris (2018)	*2,140,526*	*40.7*
Manila (2010)	1,652,171	16.6
Barcelona (2017)	*1,620,809*	*39.2*
Dallas (2017)	1,341,075	340.9

APPENDIX B

Singapore Accolades

The following is a short list of some of the accolades or recognitions that Singapore has achieved on a worldwide level over the last few years.

- Most "Technology-Ready" Nation
- Top International Meetings City
- World's Smartest City
- World's Safest Country
- Most Expensive City to live in since 2013
- Maritime Capital (Port of Singapore)
- Best Airport (Changi Airport)
- Best Airline (Singapore Airlines - 2018)
- 2nd Busiest Container Port
- 3rd Least Corrupt Country
- 3rd Largest Financial Center

Four Official Languages are spoken: English, Malay, Mandarin Chinese, and Tamil

90% of the homes are owner-occupied

39% of the residents (including permanent) are Foreign Nationals

WARREN'S BIO

Warren G. Landrum, Jr. is an Award-Winning Author, Editor, Poet, Air Force veteran, Community Activist, Alpha Phi Alpha fraternity member, Big Brother, Husband, Dad, and Grandfather who was born in East Chicago, Indiana and currently resides in Grand Prairie, Texas.

Warren has written and published seven books:

"The Heart & Soul of a Black Man"

"Let's Go Home to Indiana Harbor: Reflections From Mid-Town America"

"Texas Politics – Grand Prairie Style: Campaign 2013"

"The Stroke of Grace:
Trauma, Triumph and Testimony of Former NBA Player Juaquin "Hawk" Hawkins"

"Nine Days in Italy:
The Highs and Lows of Driving Through Italia"(3rd-Place Winner in Adult Non-Fiction category at 2018 North Texas Book Festival in Denton, TX,) which he co-wrote with his wife Carol,

"Nine Days in Paris:
The Journey Continues" (2nd-Place Winner in Adult Non-Fiction category at 2019 North Texas Book Festival)

and his first Children's Book,

"Mia Goes to Jamaica: An ABC Journey."

This book, "Nine Days in Singapore…", joins "Nine Days in Italy…" and "Nine Days in Paris…" in Warren's Travel Series.

Contact info:
warrenglandrum@hotmail.com
Cell: 682-351-6516
Website: www.warlandbooks.com

www.ingramcontent.com/pod-product-compliance
Lightning Source LLC
Chambersburg PA
CBHW051550010526
44118CB00022B/2646